What We Keep

poems by

Rosalie Sanara Petrouske

Finishing Line Press
Georgetown, Kentucky

What We Keep

Copyright © 2016 by Rosalie Sanara Petrouske
ISBN 978-1-944251-65-9   First Edition
All rights reserved under International and Pan-American Copyright Conventions.
No part of this book may be reproduced in any manner whatsoever without written permission from the publisher, except in the case of brief quotations embodied in critical articles and reviews.

ACKNOWLEDGMENTS

Grateful acknowledgment is made to the editors of the following publications in which these poems, or versions of these poems first appeared:

Publications
The Antigonish Review, "Hollyhocks."
Driftwood, "The Alchemy of Air."
Garfield Lake Review, "Burnt."
Parting Gifts, "Life Pressed."
Passages North, "Jealousies."
The MacGuffin, "In the World Tonight."
The Pre-Press Awards, Volume II, "Pyrotechnics."
Third Wednesday, "Lepidoptera," "Crusts," "Lilacs."
Southern Poetry Review, "Moon Through an Amber Glass."
Sweet Annie Press and Sweet Pea Review, Eclectic Woman, "Walking with My Unborn Daughter," "Strawberry Lake."

Anthologies
New Poems from the Third Coast: Contemporary Michigan Poetry, edited by Conrad Hillberry, Josie Kearns and Michael Delp: "Moon Through an Amber Glass."

Chapbooks
A Postcard from My Mother, Finishing Line Press, 2004: "My Daughter Learns," "Deadman's Float," "Strawberry Lake," "Walking with My Unborn Daughter," and "Lilacs."

The Geisha Box, March Street Press, 1996: "Hollyhocks," "Jealousies."

Competitions
Abbie M. Copps Poetry Award, 2012: First Honorable Mention, "Burnt."

Editor: Christen Kincaid
Cover Art: Bonnie Bucqueroux
Author Photo: Roxanne J. Frith
Cover Design: Elizabeth Maines

Printed in the USA on acid-free paper.
Order online: www.finishinglinepress.com
also available on amazon.com

Author inquiries and mail orders:
Finishing Line Press
P. O. Box 1626
Georgetown, Kentucky 40324
U. S. A.

Table of Contents

Spells for a Traveler 1

Moon Through an Amber Glass 3

My Daughter Learns 5

Life Pressed 7

Yellow Autumn 8

Hollyhocks 10

Pyrotechnics 11

Burnt 12

Driving Through Fog the Day after Thanksgiving 13

Crusts 14

Jealousies 15

Lilacs 16

Dead-man's Float 17

Strawberry Lake 18

Walking with My Unborn Daughter 20

Lepidoptera 21

Invisible 22

Along the River Tonight 23

The Alchemy of Air 25

In the World Tonight 26

Regrets Noir 28

Always, for Senara

Spells for a Traveler

I.

Mother believed in spells to keep us safe.
The night before our long drive
to Wisconsin, she said,
"Henry, please take the St. Christopher to St. Pat's,
and have it blessed."

I waited in the car with Mother,
while Father slipped carefully through the church door,
discreet like a robber or secret lover,
hoping to remain anonymous.
Faint light glowed behind stained glass
offering comfort to the faithful.

I imagined him hiding in a corner of the vestibule,
leaning into shadows, watching the last parishioners
leave after attending evening mass.
I saw the priest's black winged sleeve reaching down,
      his hand stretching out in supplication,
long fingers dipping into holy water,
then touching the silver disc reverently
before raising it to his lips,
as he intoned God's mysterious language.

What words could he possibly speak to keep us safe
as we drove toward our destination?
What words stop the drunken driver from veering into our lane?
Or keep a sleeping semi-trucker from steering all of us into oblivion?
From what mortal dangers could those incantations offer protection?
Bridges downed by flooded rivers, black ice, nights without stars?

Back then, I never understood my mother's faith:
she clung to such insignificant gestures,
yet rebelled at baptizing her youngest daughter.

When he returned, Father placed the blessed medal in her palm.
Relieved, she pinned it to the visor, as we turned onto US 41.

He drove all night through Wisconsin farmland while I slept.
The St. Christopher hovered above his steady hands,
    guiding us toward morning.

II.

This winter their granddaughter learns to drive.
When I know it's stormy up north where she lives,
I think of those icy roads along Lake Superior—
Lake-effect snow obliterates center lines and rumble strips.
Even fog sometimes rolls off the bay,
so thick it moors iron ore boats for days.
There she drives down hilly inclines, pumping brakes,
downshifting, passing without passing lanes.

I need spells for my own traveler, a St. Christopher
for her dashboard, a blessing from the Pope.
Although untutored in the proper way to pray,
I repeat, *"God, keep her safe. Let her wheels glide
with ease, let her maneuver each curve the way
she handled her spiraling kite as a child,
giving its string just enough length so it caught
    the wind at right angles
        and soared.
If she begins to slide, let her turn into the skid,
never touch her brakes, and steer, steer, steer."*

Moon Through an Amber Glass

My father studied the moon through an amber glass.
He knew the sailor's warning about red skies,
the North Star as compass—I know some of my father.

He was gray-haired, over fifty at my birth.
I am told he rocked me, slapped my back at croup,
floorboards creaking and perhaps I recall the songs—
but I'm not sure. It feels like I've known only women
all my life, those figures that hover in aprons
and good advice, warmed by fresh-baked bread, white
potatoes, gravy drippings, and smelling of sun-dried sheets.

When I was three my father pulled me away from
the drunken neighbor who tried to take me to his house,
struck that younger man's face until it bounced
like a bloodied ball. This scene is clear to me.
I feared him then, but afterwards with fists
still bleeding, he rocked me until my trembling stopped.

The women in my family raised their voices.
It took my father longer to anger—to meet that shrillness
with his rage. He was an old man who talked about
the geography of the earth, the molten layers
and sedimentary rocks moved by wind and rain.
When I ran high fevers, he walked to St. Francis,
asked the nuns for pills to break fevers, to save
the life of his little girl.

He carved a wooden cross for my older sister,
Rose-Marie, who was born a "blue baby."
He named me after his favorite niece,
the girl that worked at a five and dime,
and died from a brain tumor at seventeen.
I grew up believing I would never reach
my eighteenth birthday.

In my only picture of my father as a young man,
he wears a gray suit, his shirt collar starched
high and white, his gray felt Homburg at an angle
to his broad forehead.

In that photograph, I do not recognize the man
I knew at Stonington who covered a wasp sting
      in my palm with his mouth,
              and pulled the poison into him.

My Daughter Learns

Premature, my daughter was yanked into the stiff air and
    swaddled.
It was four days before she knew her mother's flesh.
Groping blindly she sought the curve of my cheek.
I was a fever radiating to her small fingers.
So I wrapped her in the nakedness of mother and father,
entwined in arms, against breasts and chest during her first winter.

I show my daughter colors—
At first she discerned only light and dark—shapes
dominated by my face. Then she resounded
with joyful trills at the red bowl, her own hand,
the slope of light on her father's nose—
my daughter's first seeing.

At eight months she learns touch like the blind,
spreading her hands over objects, over my eyebrows
and lips, greedy for sensations.

She pushes her tongue across my palm—sucks
at the salt of my skin. *Daughter*, I tell her, *this is good.*
She pushes her own fingers into her mouth, startles
herself with their sweetness.

Her first bites of tangerine, of quince, of ripe cherry.
What a delight! All this to choose from, all this to savor—
    tartness,
honey, and brine. She pushes her tongue forward, over her lip,
licks. There will be many firsts, I tell her—tongue to snow, to
    rain,
to the curves of a lover's back, and essences to inhale.
Yes, daughter, take great gulps of the world.

Her infant voice rises in pure notes—halves of scales
that reach out and test the air. She cocks her head to listen
for scraps of noise—the scratching of winter moles,
whirring of rain-slapped streets.

I form words around my tongue for her—teach her
to mimic the Oh's and Ah's, the beginning of her voice
calling out above her crib at night to the round
moon face; I can teach her lilting rhythms, senseless
rhymes, but she must let it spill into the air,
      that mysterious shape—

her first word.

Life Pressed

In the book I am reading,
I turn a page,
find a brown spider pressed—
wonder how this small house spider
ended up here? Long ago,
I collected flowers and leaves
with my grandmother. She held
my hand while I smoothed
the fragrant petals,
placed them between
pages of a Montgomery Ward catalog.
Somewhere in the basement,
a box holds one of my old scrapbooks,
the cardboard kind with gold filigree edging
and a knotted string like a shoelace
holding its cover together.
I showed it to my daughter once,
the crumbly oak leaves, blue bell-shaped flowers
my grandmother called harebells, orange butterfly
weed and white meadowsweet.
The flowers are so old now,
their edges outlined in yellow, crooked
silhouettes of nature—if you touched one
it would surely dissolve into dust
like the spider does when it falls from my book
and lands amongst the crumbs
of the scone I am eating.

Yellow Autumn

"It's a yellow autumn," he says, and is right.
The elms, aspen, and tamaracks have turned tints of amber,
even the maples boast more golden hues than shades of red.
We rake leaves in crisp Michigan air,
side by side—moving back and forth,
our arms sometimes brushing, the sleeve of my sweater
touching the sleeve of his flannel shirt.
I am sixteen; my father seventy-four.
As he bends to scrape a clump of leaves from the tines
of his rake, his white hair lifts in the wind.
His forearms are muscled from years of pounding nails,
lifting beams, sliding a saw deep into rough bark,
or running a plane over a plank of pine
until it shimmers with smoothness. I never think him old,
even when kids who don't know me ask if he is my grandfather.
We have been working for hours.
He smiles down at me. "Are you getting tired?"
"No," I say and mean it.
I could do this until the snow begins to fall, ground freezes.
Our pile of gold is waist deep, smells of damp earth.
When I was little, I jumped in head first.
He buried me until only the tassel on my red hat stuck out.
Mother yelled at him to stop.
"You're getting her clothes all dirty," she said.
I'm too old now to jump in piles of leaves.
I've already kissed three boys;
one touched my breasts.
Of course, my father doesn't know this.
"Let's take a break," he says, opens the thermos
and we sit, backs against the oak, drink coffee,
no cream or sugar. We share one cup
between us, back and forth—sip and sip,
wrap our hands around the rim to warm them.
The October air smells like wood smoke and cinnamon,
clings to our hair and clothes. When I finally go to sleep
tonight with aching shoulders, blistered palms,

I'll still smell the wood smoke in my hair and on my pillow.
I want this afternoon to last, notice the sun slipping
        lower—
I'm happy, I realize, surprised,
lean my head against his arm.
We stare out at the woods, beyond to a hidden creek;
light slants through branches—sunglow.
It almost hurts our eyes.
There is no way to know in another week
my father will die from a heart attack,
while sanding the fallen trunk of a mulberry tree
for a bench he is making my mother and me.

Hollyhocks

Christine was the Polish girl who lived next door.
She was a year older.
Her clothes always smelled of cooked cabbage
    and *kielbasa*.
During fire drills at Lincoln school,
we shared smiles across opposite stairwells.
We used to kiss the clothes poles in my backyard,
pretend they were our boyfriends.
Cold afternoons when school let out,
we stood in Wojakowski's drugstore,
smelled the licorice and horehound
drops, stared with greedy eyes
at the tray of cut-glass rings.
I lived in the corner house with
my sister and her husband.
Her husband always screamed at me
for pulling silver threads
out of their red davenport
with my shoe buckles.
Once I accidentally sneezed
on an airmail envelope
by the supper table.
He went into the living room,
sat in the dark while his food
grew cold.
In the spring, Christine and I played
hopscotch and tag around an oak
that pushed crookedly out of
the playground's blacktop.
We named it the witch's tree,
carved our childish messages
into its reluctant bark.
In the summer we dreamed among
the hollyhocks that stood high
as the backyard fence,
spilled their purple, red and white
flowers to dazzle our eyes
where ten years later Christine made
love to boys in the backseats of their cars.

Pyrotechnics

I hated the idea of washing one man's shirts
all my life, having supper at exactly six o' clock.
There had to be fireworks, pinwheels and starbursts.

Grandmother told me when she looked at two people,
she could always tell if there were sparks,
if that couple would grow old together. I wanted sparks.

Uncle Joe worked in the firecracker factory,
sent off those bursting missiles on the Fourth of July,
blazoned the night with fire. It was indeed an art for
Uncle Joe, igniting the sky brighter than the summer stars.

He told me about the compounds that defined each color—
strontium for red; copper, blue; barium, green; and sodium, yellow.
They also use magnesium and aluminum powder to add
         extra flash, he said.

When Uncle Joe died, he had his ashes rolled in the paper
of a starburst—sent them all the way to Lake Louise.
It was the best fireworks display in a decade.

My sister believes in being satisfied with the way things are.
I was a funny kid. On the Fourth of July, the fireworks
never lasted long enough for me. God, how I'd howl!
The whole park could hear me even down to where
the tuba player was sleeping in the bandshell.

I wonder sometimes,
am I the only one who understands?
I know enough now to realize
not everything is light, noise and smoke,
but I'm still searching for the trip wire
that will illuminate the dark.

Burnt

Everything withered, the pear flowers
shriveled like onion leaves.
The grass beneath my bare heels
crackles as if I were stepping
on sheaves of dried corn.
My prize lily, blooming madly in June,
when the fireflies dipped
into its abundant petals
has wilted to a few crumpled leaves,
an emaciated stalk.
Rain, rain,
the blue jay screeches.
Rain whispers
the willow,
even the river is too low
to paddle.
I am grateful for the moths
thumping at the midnight pane,
for the night-flying bat.
I almost hear the earth
absorbing darkness,
the distant whistle as the train
clatters over the bridge,
trusses creaking and swaying
beneath its weight.
No breath of wind stirs a leaf.
Dry, so dry,
my mouth
thirsts for a drink,
my lips
hurt,
sore and waiting
for the kiss of water,
and my heart beats
fast and hard.
I feel it sear
with all the longing,
all the want
of a lifetime.

Driving Through Fog the Day after Thanksgiving

We travel all night turned toward home.
You complain the oncoming headlights
hurt your eyes, swerve over the white line
once, twice. Do you want me to drive? I ask.
No. . . . no. Mercury lights on pole barns,
lamps in windows of farmhouses,
brightly lit gas stations blink and disappear.
After Wisconsin, it begins to rain.
I doze to old rock and roll tunes on the radio,
wake to see you flinch when a truck pulls up behind,
its high beams glaring into the side view mirrors.
I ask what's wrong. "Nothing," you say.
But you always say that.
So I chatter about inconsequential things,
who will unpack the car, get the dog,
stop at the neighbor's tomorrow morning
to ask for our mail. You nod and squint harder,
hunched over the wheel.
I turn away and look out at the darkness speeding by.
We never talk anymore about what we find beautiful;
a turn of phrase, a perfect blue iris, or stand
on the porch and breathe in summer rain.
You never come to look when I tell you the first fireflies
are out, or listen when I read a new poem aloud.
The doctor says you need an operation on your eyes;
this is why you cannot see at night,
why halos encircle globes of streetlights.
We have been driving through fog for a long time.

Crusts

It's like picking at a scab,
the kind that covers a burn
with the skin underneath red,
tender, a raw wound.

Once I collected oysters
at Puget sound.
After they dried on the windowsill,
the dead animals rattled inside.
When I tried to pry them open—
they cracked.

It's like throwing chunks of week-old bread
to the geese at the river.
They consume it, insatiable,
sometimes choking on the hard crusts.
I'm like that now—tearing at the layers
of your words, scratching until I draw blood.

Jealousies

1.

My father wore a Homburg hat,
powdered his face with fine white powder.
My mother raged when women
spoke to him on the street.

Once he threw the pictures
from his wallet into the snow.
Before he scuffed them under with his boot,
I saw a photograph of a dark-haired girl.
I was afraid to ask my father who she was.

Under the faded ironing board cover,
my mother still keeps a Valentine
he gave her in nineteen sixty-six.
On the front of the card,
a big-breasted girl poses
in a tight red dress.
My mother would not speak to him
for a week after.

2.

Sometimes I do not call first
before I come home early from work.
I look for changes in my lover's expression
when he thinks I am not watching him,
for scraps of hair in my comb.
Last night I looked
between all the photos in his wallet.

I count the little jealousies,
carry them with me, take them out fondly
and stroke their heads until they purr.

Lilacs

I.

In May everything was light as air.
You filled my arms with lilacs. I stood tiptoe
to gather them from your hands. One bloom
held a hidden bee that stung my cheek.

Sometimes, I still hate you, Mother.
You made me afraid of the water—
telling me that blueness would close over
my face, pinching back my breath like a fold of skin,
before pulling me into its depths—
I still don't swim.

When your heart failed, you rocked your swollen legs
for hours, refused to wear the sweater I gave you
for Christmas, to read the books I checked out of the library.
Your lungs drowned in an ocean. I imagined the color of lilacs—
all purplish-blue, budding over your heart.

II.

This spring I walk down the hill into a lake
of lilacs. I think of you picking armfuls of white,
lavender, and magenta, filling the kitchen with lilac
perfume. I hear you singing,
></br>*"Down by the seashore, Mary Ann,
down by the seashore sifting sand."*

I pick lilacs for you, wanting only
to feel your thin shoulders beneath my palms,
to enclose you in my arms like those fragrant boughs.
I fill every room in my house with lilacs singing
*"Down by the seashore, Mary Ann,
down by the seashore sifting sand."*

I tell everyone my mother loved lilacs.

Dead-man's Float

Wood smoke and leaf-rot
bring me into this season.
Again, I am the child lithe enough
to dive from the front steps
into leaves of copper, red, gold,
my mother telling me,
"the leaves are dirty, dirty."

I think of a cool lake
where she was afraid
to let me wade up to my knees.
Her story of Carp Lake told over and over,
a sudden squall, her parents' rowboat tossed.
So I never learned to paddle into all that blue,
to practice the dead-man's float.

Mother admired bodies of water
from their shores, kept her white legs dry.
I can still see her stroking leaves with a wooden
fan rake, her arms strong as any swimmer's.

Strawberry Lake

It is October; the month of my father's dying.
At Strawberry Lake, the water is so still
nothing moves in that blue except for one trout
    startled.
It leaps so high it sends out a circle of ripples that
    spin
across the water to the feet of my daughter.
At two, she is inquisitive, chasing the autumn
    brown
grasshoppers that move slowly at her intrusion—
    leap
over blackened stems of mushrooms.

All around us the lake is rimmed with fire, color so
bright it hurts the eyes: maple, poplar, hemlock
and drying thistle where dragonflies
fan out their wings,
land and drink of leftover nectar.

I take my daughter's hand to walk around the lake.
She is a miracle—this independent child
who watches me out of my own eyes.
Everything is new to her.
I tell her, "jack pine," "moss," "cricket,"
and she repeats each word,
testing the syllables like trout
breaking the surface in clean, swift strides.
We are inventing the language here
at Strawberry Lake.
She listens to the crickets in the brush.
"They are lamenting the end of summer," I tell her.

My mother loved crickets,
their lonely cries as they sought
winter mates—my mother dead of bone cancer
when I was thirty-two,
my mother who said good-bye long before
her final departure.
She gave me the fragrance of lilacs
to bury my face into,

the taste of wintergreen pulled from the earth
to place on my tongue—
these were the small epiphanies she loved.
She told me never to expect too much
and I would not be disappointed.

A sign at the edge of the lake says anglers
can only use artificial lures with a single hook,
can only take two trout per day. They must throw
back any fish less than fifteen inches.
Under that clear surface,
I imagine trout growing longer than my arms and legs,
sliding their silver bellies over the rocky bottom,
only sending the young to flirt with the anglers' bait.

I watch my daughter run forward.
She seems to be growing
taller even as I stare,
and I cannot put out my hand to stop
her forward motion any more
than I can prevent the leaves from spiraling down.
She darts toward the water,
her feet propelling her like fins.
Stop! I want to scream.
Instead, I remain silent,
reach the water's edge before her,
raise her into my arms.

In the bones of my daughter's face, I see my
    mother,
my father repeated—and this is something to
    celebrate
like the song of the insects, the buzz of a
    lethargic bee—
this glorious color promising a burst of
    brilliance before fading
into the dimness of November.

My daughter's breath mingles with my own
as I carry her away. We leave Strawberry Lake
    behind, reeling in the golden light.

Walking with My Unborn Daughter

I walk into the wind along the lake
breathing in the season as it folds its wings
around me like the great Cecropia moth
that once cast its shadow over the light
on my grandmother's back porch.

The child inside me moves, flutter-kicks
and pauses, a soft rising, as if she is rolling
over, twirling like a bright leaf in its final flight,
but her movements are only beginning.

Beneath my feet the cement poured last summer
has captured the shape of maple leaves,
flawless in their descent.
I touch an imprint with my toe.
Daughter, what impressions will you make?
I wonder. *What will be impressed upon you?*

A friend once told me that the longer we live,
the harder it becomes to decide
what to let go of, what to keep.
My body rocks slowly, a ship at quiet anchor.
What are you thinking, daughter?
I ask the wind moving through the oaks.
What will you someday keep of me?

Lepidoptera

The cigar box lined with cotton, held seven butterflies,
thoraxes pierced by black enameled pins,

a Monarch, Viceroy, Swallowtail, Red Admiral,
Great Spangled Fritillary, Painted Lady, Mourning Cloak,

all in flight, wings spread catching an updraft of breeze
gliding over thistles, landing on a birch leaf.

Wind in the grass keened like an old man
those summer afternoons while

my father built a spreading board from cork and balsa wood,
helped me with the killing jar, the long handled net.

If I were careless, their scales smudged my fingertips,
left tracings of colored powder I wiped on my jeans.

In the jar the butterflies looked out with compound eyes
beyond to the field filled with milkweed, violets, elderberries,

uncoiled their proboscis, felt the glass.
What is it like to breathe in carbon tetrachloride?

Sometimes it took them all night to die;
in the morning wings clasped still and stiff.

Years later, after the drive to Lawrence,
when I opened the cigar box,

those butterfly wings shattered into their base elements,
into dust, that scattered across the ground and lifted

into a warm Kansas wind.

Invisible
>*(for Janice)*

Twenty years now,
you have been gone.
Hundreds of Perseid meteor showers
have streaked the skies on lonely midnights.
Scientists have invented an invisibility cloak
that hides objects in the visible spectrum of light.
Perhaps, you could have hid from the world
under its protective layers, its golden particles
evaporating around you—here you are,
then no longer discernible to anyone looking.
February is cold this year—so much snow,
just like long ago when we caught snowflakes
on our tongues, turned our faces to the wide sky
and let frigid air fill our lungs.
Ice has collected on the branches and light
arcs from those splinters.
        It hurts my eyes.

The last time I saw your son, he was twelve.
He's a man now, perhaps has children of his own.
As a child, he always hid under blankets, behind curtains,
in piles of leaves, thinking no one could see him.
You always knew where he was, though.
I wonder if he is still hiding, waiting for you to find him,
or does he think you forgot to look?

I open the back door of my house, reach out
to gather all this sparkling light into my arms,
wish I could still wrap my arms around you,
tell you, it will be all right, tell you
        I will disappear with you,
        if you wish it so.

Along the River Tonight

Along the river tonight, darkness deepens—
Overhead, a not quite oval moon
reflects in water where geese rest,
wings folded as they float.

Couples walk paved paths touching hands.
Tree frogs throw out their throaty opera.
Here in mid-summer, first crickets begin their
song, rubbing legs frantically against each other.

Next to me, my daughter walks slowly,
head down, hands tucked in pockets,
thoughts far away, up north at the big lake
where soon she travels to her father's home.

I want her to love the Grand, to be familiar with this
water the same way she knows Superior, and
      recognizes
its cobalt blueness as it rises to meet the horizon.
I can tell her what I have learned about lakes.

I'm just learning the mysteries of rivers.
Lakes have no tides, yet rivers rush.
Toss a stone into a lake and it is lost:
Toss a stone into a river; it skips and awakens ripples.

In the upper reach amongst swift water
algae clings to rock, smooth—polished
almost black by rubbing of water and time.
Evergreen, moss, pine—this is the river's color.

Trout feed on larvae of stoneflies, wait
for anglers' hooks to find them. Dippers perch
on river stones, search for food to feed their young.
There is danger here as well as beauty.

In the middle reach, water moves slowly—
Notice how plants put down stocky roots,
snails hide in weeds and under stones.
Largemouth bass propel to safety,

a fleeting flash of silver caught only by discerning eyes.
Now in the lower reach, we watch
dragonflies hover, glassy wings paper thin,
translucent enough to see through.
Each wing glistens bits of shattered light.

Some rivers are straight; others meander,
carving out land as they travel onwards.
I have lived my life by water: lakes and rivers,
waterfalls bursting with anticipation.

Some rivers are quiet, unpredictable,
others cold and turbulent,
except for mallards sheltering under bridges,
hid beneath willow fronds.

It is almost dark now as we walk along the Grand.
At thirteen, my daughter grows stalky
and thin as cattails,
bending in the swampy areas beyond this path.

It is easy to love a daughter too much,
with a heart overflowing its banks
like the river after snow melts in March.

People say that love is great ambition;
it curls under skin like mud under fingernails,
eddies around you, grabs at wrists and ankles
like fast-flowing water, can pull you beneath the
       surface,

and all you can do is hold on. . . . hold on.

The Alchemy of Air

The alchemist knows the secret of dying, how the last breath
    sails up like smoke, a white cloud of birds,
or steam rising from water.
I felt my mother sigh against my palm,
    wondered if her spirit lifted to the rafters
of the green hospital room.
I wound her fingers around my own,
    spoke spells for her safe journey.
Sublimatio, the alchemists call this.
    Dickinson's "soul at white heat."
When she let go of my hand,
    I opened my mouth
to call her back.
    No sound escaped, only a soft
hiss of air brushed past me
    in the hushed room.

In the World Tonight

The world is round and warm tonight
redolent with scents of fresh cut grass,
sweet clover, mock orange, corn
tasseling toward mid-summer. Senara,
my twelve-year-old daughter, is camping
with her father at Lake of the Clouds. I wait
for her to call, say she misses me, but she does not.

I run my hand along the silent phone the way
I used to stroke her long, smooth hair. I imagine
her now climbing the Escarpment trail in moonlight,
pulling her pack high across her back, her father
stopping to point out the moon rising over hemlocks
to ripple its thin light across water below.

Here the recently mowed Creeping Charlie
sends up its aroma, minty and sharp, mixed
with the fragrance of roses growing at the fence.
My aloneness closes over me when first fireflies appear.
I shut my eyes and breathe in the coming dark.

Senara and her father will raise the tent, roll out
sleeping bags, and collect kindling for a fire.
A black bear nearby will rustle in the brambles
rummaging for food. They'll stare up at the sky
littered with stars, night insects roaring in their ears.
It's a sound like no other, like wind lifting upper
pine branches or hissing through cracks in rocks.

Here, there are other kinds of sounds—moth wings
fluttering against streetlamps, late bird chorus
in the blue spruce—their final evening song
before folding wings to rest. As it grows darker,
I sit on the back deck with my dog, an arm
around his soft neck, and watch stars come out.

I embrace my solitude the way the single white pine
in our yard gathers a silence of light in its branches,
the way a small rabbit ventures out before
hopping into a yew hedge. Even the sphinx moths

clustered against our tattered screen door
appear lonely, trumpeting their wings,
flying off one by one searching for a porch
with brighter illumination.

When my daughter comes home, she'll tell me
how they climbed higher, looked down through
a stand of old growth hemlocks to watch
morning mist rise off the lake. It seemed like
we were floating in the clouds, she'll say,
then describe their hike to Trapper's Falls,
water so clean you could drink it.

My father wants me to come here,
spread his ashes someday when he dies.
I think, how kind, how wonderful to tumble
over smooth rock winding down through
the mountain, become part of our earth.
This I learn after she returns.

For tonight, I have a dog and a star-filled sky,
legs that stretch, and my sun-browned hands
for stroking my dog's ears. So, who am I to complain?
What luck to be alive in the world tonight.

Regrets Noir

The long days of November
are shuttered in grayness,
a bit of snow here and
my breath clamors with ice.
I slowly breathe in and out.
The sluggish river
flows listlessly down
to the dam.

The sky, a dark net,
hovers over this landscape
spilling pellets of sharp rain.
Only a few crumpled leaves cling
to a branch of cottonwood
and the willow's long tendrils
have dried and bronzed,
though now are beaded with water.

I walk the river's edge, sodden earth
squishing beneath my boots.
The dog pulls at his leash,
looking around aimlessly.
Not even a squirrel scurries over
dormant limbs above our heads,
no mallards skim water as they rise.
Through this downcast world,
hope twangs a tentative string—
I dread the burden of winter still ahead,
this darkness suddenly falling as quickly
as the temperature.

What's yet to be, I wonder?
What's left behind?
There's not much I can change,
or undo; an apology never spoken,
a ticket lost, a diamond ring slipped
on a finger while snow
falls inside a glass dome,

skipping at midnight
holding a lover's hand.
All this a part of me; all this lost.
The missed and the missing.

I enter a silent house,
dry my dog's black fur,
shake dampness from my matted hair.
My daughter calls
from another time zone,
her voice lilts like
a melodious piano key
pressed and held.
I could listen all night,
but she only wants me
to send a bottle of strawberry
shampoo.

I curl into the overstuffed chair
with the dog at my feet.
Tires of cars beyond my window
whoosh past on a wet road.
Everything beats in synchronization
with the slow thump of my heart.
What would I change if I could? I ask again.
Nothing, nothing, nothing, is the reply.
There is hot tea, a plaid blanket,
pen and paper
to celebrate.

Rosalie Sanara Petrouske spends her time walking along the Grand River near her Victorian home in the small town of Grand Ledge, Michigan. Her black lab is often her companion. She has published poetry and essays in many literary journals, anthologies, and two chapbooks. Recently, she was the featured poet in *Third Wednesday* and, in 2015, appeared as the April/May poet in a broadside for the *Michigan Poet*. She has also served twice as Artist-in-Residence in the Porcupine Mountains wilderness area in Michigan's Upper Peninsula. Images of the natural world are prominent throughout her work as she stays true to the teachings of her Ojibwe father, who taught her how to provide careful stewardship and to always honor her surrounding environment, whether a woodland or urban landscape.